The
3 PEAI

C000122481

The Official

BEN NEVIS - SCOTLAND
SCAFELL PIKE - ENGLAND
SNOWDON - WALES

ONE BOOK COVERING 3 MOUNTAINS
Also including information on the UK's
4th Peak – Slieve Donard - N. Ireland

AN
ESSENTIAL GUIDE TO
HELP YOU COMPLETE
THE
NATIONAL 3 PEAKS WALK

BRIAN G. SMAILES

Brian Smailes

Holds the record for the fastest 4 and 5 continuous crossings of the Lyke Wake Walk over the North York Moors. He completed the 210 miles over rough terrain on 5 crossings in June 1995 taking 85 hours and 50 minutes. In 2008 he completed his 53rd crossing.

An expedition in 2008 took him to the jungles around Canaima in Venezuela, exploring on foot and by dugout canoe the tributaries of the Rio Carrao up to Angel Falls. China's Great Wall expedition in 2007 involved walking sections in remote areas along the former borders of Mongolia. On a 2005 expedition, Brian walked the Inca Trail in Peru, visiting Lake Titticacca and Bolivia while in the area.

In August 2003 he walked from John O'Groats to Lands End, completing it in 34 days. In August 2001 he cycled from Lands End to John O`Groats, a journey of over 910 miles in 6 days 13 hours 18 minutes. This involved carrying food, clothing and tent, and was completed without support between both ends. A further cycle ride, this time from John O'Groats to Lands End took place in July 2007 to complete the two way cycle crossing.

Having travelled extensively throughout the UK, Europe and the Caribbean, Brian has recently been writing international travel guides to enable the holidaymaker to access the world with ease and enjoy it as much as he does.

Long distance running, canoeing and sub aqua diving are other sports he enjoys, completing 25 marathons and canoeing the Caledonian Canal 3 times. Brian has dived all around the UK coastline as well as Thailand, Cuba, Venezuela, Egypt and Mexico.

Brian lives in Yorkshire and has walked the hills and dales throughout the County. In compiling this 4th edition of The National 3 Peaks Walk, the route still holds as much pleasure now as it did the first time he walked it.

Walk Guides

THE YORKSHIRE DALES TOP TEN
ISBN 978-0-9526900-5-4

THE DERBYSHIRE TOP TEN
ISBN 978-1-903568-03-3

THE COMPLETE ISLE OF WIGHT COASTAL FOOTPATH
ISBN 978-0-9526900-6-1

ISLE OF WIGHT, NORTH TO SOUTH – EAST TO WEST
ISBN 978-1-903568-07-1

THE SCOTTISH COAST TO COAST WALK
ISBN 978-0-9526900-8-5

THE LYKE WAKE WALK GUIDE
ISBN 978-1-903568-47-7

THE YORKSHIRE 3 PEAKS WALK
SKETCH MAP & ROUTE GUIDE
ISBN 978-1-903568-23-1

20 WALKS AROUND GLEN NEVIS & FORT WILLIAM
ISBN 978-1-903568-57-6

THE GREAT GLEN WAY
ISBN 978-1-903568-13-2

THE LANCASHIRE TRAIL
ISBN 978-1-903568-10-1

THE 1066 COUNTRY WALK
ISBN 978-1-903568-00-2

THE NOVICES GUIDE TO THE YORKSHIRE 3 PEAKS WALK
ISBN 978 1-903568-46-0

SHORT WALKS IN THE LAKE DISTRICT
ISBN 978-1-903568-20-0

JOHN O'GROATS TO LANDS END
ISBN 978-1-903568-18-7

WALK HADRIAN'S WALL
ISBN 978-1-903568-40-8

Tourist Guide
EXPLORE – FORT WILLIAM & GLEN NEVIS
ISBN 978-1-903568-25-5

Cycling Guide
LANDS END TO JOHN O'GROATS
ISBN 978-1-903568-11-8

Obtainable from bookshops or direct from the address or web site below. See web site for book details -

www.chall-pub.co.uk
or **www.national3peaks.co.uk**

THE NATIONAL 3 PEAKS WALK
ISBN 978-1-903568-53-8
Fourth Edition - 2009

CHALLENGE PUBLICATIONS
7, EARLSMERE DRIVE, BARNSLEY. S71 5HH

ACKNOWLEDGEMENTS

It is with thanks to the following people for assistance, that this book has been published: -

Pam Smailes.

Location Photographs - Brian Smailes.

Graphic Design - Jamie Mann.

Clothing & Equipment - Berghaus "Extrem" Range.

Brian Smailes is identified as author of this book in accordance with Copyright Act 1988.

First Published	1996
Second Edition	2000
Third Edition	2005
Fourth Edition	2009

ISBN 978-1-903568-53-8

Published by Challenge Publications,
7, Earlsmere Drive, Ardsley, Barnsley, S71 5HH.
www.chall-pub.co.uk
www.national3peaks.co.uk

CONTENTS

PHOTOGRAPHS

PREFACE TO THE 4th EDITION

The routes described in this book are written for walkers who either choose to take up the 3 peaks 24-hour challenge or to climb each peak at a more enjoyable leisurely pace. There is no rule that says you must complete the 3 peaks in 24 hours. Peaks can be climbed over days, weeks or years. Trying to do this in 24 hours leads to loss of enjoyment and a higher risk of accidents.

The effort required to complete the National 3 Peaks cannot be under estimated. The lack of proper sleep, food and comfort does take its toll on people of all ages, particularly those in mid life and over, which is the average age of the long distance walker.

"One of the ultimate challenges in the United Kingdom" is how many people describe this 3 peaks walk. Ben Nevis at 1344m, Scafell Pike at 978m and Snowdon at 1085m. The challenge of climbing the 3 highest mountains in Great Britain appeals to many walkers. Included in this edition is the information for those who would like to tackle a 4th peak, Slieve Donard in Northern Ireland. This is situated in the Mourne Mountains and is 850m in height.

This book looks at preparation, walking and driving routes to use on this classic walk. The inclusion of campsites and B&Bs for each area should prove a valuable help. Sketch maps have been included to use in conjunction with the relevant map. The photographs give an accurate representation of the spectacular scenery and the conditions that can be encountered on the 3 peaks.

Following the advice given in this book, which includes new and updated information, should enable all walkers to complete the National 3 Peaks Walk in a safe and competent manner.

It gives me great pleasure to present this 4th edition of my book, to help you fulfil your ambition of walking The National 3 Peaks Walk!

Brian Smailes

THREE PEAKS ADVENTURE

With all our equipment together

And plans that have taken weeks

We are on our way with confidence

To tackle the National Three Peaks

You can climb them in any order

So armed with map, compass and whistle

We are heading North of the border

Travelling to the land of the thistle

The first mountain we have to conquer

To test the fitness of women and men

Is the highest climb of them all

To reach the summit of The Ben

For the route to the top of Ben Nevis

We will be taking the tourist track

This is the easiest route up there

And it won't take long to get back

We will be up and down Ben Nevis

Just see how long that it takes

Before we are back in Fort William

And heading on down to The Lakes

We are now leaving The Ben behind us

Filled with anticipation we are alike

To go and climb the next mountain

And reach the summit of Scafell Pike

For the next stage of our mission

We are leaving from Wasdale Head

It is a quick and scenic route up there

At least that is what has been said

Then with Scafell Pike now completed

And all safely back down to our wagon

We are on the final stage of our journey

Heading down to the land of the dragon

For the route to the summit of Snowdon

We will take the Pyg or the Miners path

And our legs now tired and aching

Will think of a nice soak in a bath

Then all safely back to Pen-y-Pass

There is one thing we must do

That is give a special thank you

To a wonderful back up crew

Then thank God it was safely completed

And it was not just all a dream

But what made it all possible

Was the help of the back up team

Geoff Whittaker

INTRODUCTION

The National 3 Peaks of Scotland, England and Wales consist of 26 miles of ascents and descents. Weather conditions can play a big part in deciding if you can complete the walk safely. Snow, low cloud or darkness can also be deciding factors, so you need to make careful preparations, looking at the weather forecasts and the equipment that will be used for the venture.

This walk should ideally be attempted between June-Oct, the longest day being 21st June. Many people attempt the 3 peaks in June so you may well find car parks full and many other walkers around; therefore it is worth looking at other months like May, or July to September. You can of course walk it at other times of the year with caution.

In times of snow the danger of overhangs, whiteouts and false ledges can all prove fatal if you are ill prepared. Carry and know how to use essential equipment. In winter an ice axe and crampons are considered essential, as is experience and knowledge of winter conditions.

Thousands of people walk these mountains each year, some walk only one, others all three. This guide will give the information you require to complete all 3 peaks safely.

Once you gain the summit of any of these peaks you have an awesome feeling as you look out over the mountains and probably across the low cloud in the valleys and glens. This leaves a lasting impression on any walker of accomplishment, which cannot be equalled.

There are well-defined paths leading to the summits of Ben Nevis and Snowdon. Scafell Pike is slightly different, the paths are not so well defined in places, but care in planning the ascent will help you attain the summit and return safely.

The driving route between each mountain is not complicated. Although a suitable route is shown within, drivers can obviously choose their own route which they may feel is more direct or to avoid road works or other congestion.

To assist in distinguishing each area, the headings, contents and captions are colour coded throughout: -

Ben Nevis Area
Scafell Area
Snowdon Area
Slieve Donard Area
General Information

Photo 1. The start at Glen Nevis Visitor Centre

THE CHALLENGE

In 24 Hours

Start at Loch Linnhe, Fort William by touching the water at the main ferry terminal beside Crannog Sea Food Restaurant, GR.NN100738. This is near the main car park. Drive to the entrance to Glen Nevis and at the roundabout drive along Glen Nevis and park at the Visitor Centre (photo1). GR. NN123730. You now follow the route described to the summit of Ben Nevis.

After completing Ben Nevis, head south to either Wasdale Head or Seathwaite in the Lake District. Walk to the summit of Scafell Pike following one of the set routes. You may save some time by following the route from Seathwaite via the Corridor Route to Scafell Pike, returning to Wasdale Head car park (while the support vehicle drives round to Wasdale). My personal preference is to start and finish at Wasdale Head, which I feel, is more straightforward, taking only 2½ hours each way. However many people prefer the other route, which takes approx 3½ hours to ascend and can be much tougher in parts!

Once you have completed Scafell Pike, head south to Wales. Park at Pen-y-pass (charge, photo 24) or in Llanberis depending on which walking route you choose. Most people prefer to start from Pen-y-pass. Ascend to the summit of Snowdon following one of the routes described.

Your 3 peaks challenge is complete when you drive to Caernarfon Castle and touch the water at the side of the castle car park.

When attempting this challenge in 24 hours extra care should be taken because of the increased exertion required to complete in the time limit. Exhaustion can overcome you while on the mountain, and then when you stop, even for a short while, hypothermia can become a problem very quickly.

Due to the distance involved, driver fatigue is a major cause of accidents on this challenge, not to mention the speeding fines incurred as a result of trying to drive fast between each mountain as quickly as possible!

The Leisurely Alternative

As an alternative to the above challenge the 3 peaks can be walked on 3 individual days, not necessarily consecutive. In choosing this method you will have time to look around Fort William, Keswick, Llanberis or any other of the many tourist attractions on route.

Many people think this walk must be completed in 24 hours, it does not. It is probably a more rewarding experience to take your time and enjoy the once in a lifetime event.

Photo 2. One of the notice boards displaying the current weather and safety information on the 'Ben'

YOUR QUESTIONS ANSWERED

Is the walk tough?

Generally yes, but it is as tough as the amount of training you have done beforehand. The fitter you are, the easier it can be.

Can I park in Glen Nevis Camping Park grounds or use their showers?

Definitely not, unless you are resident on the site over the period you are there. The security staff will escort you off the property. The usual excuse is that walkers are doing the walk for charity, but the majority of people are. This does not give you a right to park or use their facilities and causes friction if you do. Park and start in Glen Nevis Visitor Centre car park.

Are there any shops or places to buy provisions or other items in the 3 areas?

There are no shops in the three starting areas, other than the café at Pen-y-pass (Snowdon) and the small café at Seathwaite which have normal opening times, although you may pass some on route to each destination.

How can I avoid blisters and losing toenails?

Follow my recommendations described in 'Boots & Blisters!

Are there toilets at the start of each mountain?

There are toilets at Glen Nevis Visitor Centre (photo 1) and one for customers at Seathwaite Cafe. There are none at Wasdale start but there are some for customers at Pen-y-pass Café (if open) in the car park.

Photo 3. The first gentle ascent on the lower slopes near The Ben Nevis Inn

Can I set up a checkpoint to supply our group with food etc. in Pen-y-pass car park?

No, the car park is usually full, especially weekends and because of walkers leaving litter and creating blockages in the car park, group catering is not allowed.

How can I stop my leg muscles from seizing up?

I find the best way is to get some ankle weights and wear them on the ankles around the house etc. for a few hours each day and for a few weeks before you go. Doing this will tone up those muscles. Many people wear light shoes/trainers on their feet then suddenly put on a pair of heavy boots and expect to walk up the three highest mountains, they cannot!

Where can I get badges, T-shirts, certificates etc?

Look no further. The address and web site is at the back of the book. We have a large range of quality souvenirs.

PREPARATION

This walk is not considered long compared with many other walks. Maximum distance on one mountain is 10 miles, even so if you are not prepared it could lead to problems. When preparing you need to consider the following:-

- **Fitness**
- **Food**
- **Familiarisation**
- **Equipment**

Fitness

The main problems on this walk are the steep, rugged ascents and descents especially on Ben Nevis and Scafell Pike. Because of this there is a lot of pressure on the leg muscles, knees and Achilles tendon. This pressure will considerably increase if you are attempting to climb all 3 peaks consecutively.

Exercise should be taken to build up stamina weeks ahead, i.e. walking, jogging, cycling and swimming all help to improve fitness.

Walk at an even pace, which helps to conserve energy and maintain body heat and slow release of energy. This steady pace will usually help you to overcome difficult sections without becoming exhausted. Some walkers set off at a brisk pace and often become exhausted soon afterwards. The combination of exhaustion and loss of energy can hasten the onset of hypothermia.

Food

Food consumed both before you start and while walking can affect your body heat and energy level. High-energy food such as bananas, rice, pasta, potato and wholemeal bread are all carbohydrate rich and of benefit. Eating little and often and drinking frequently is the best advice. Doing this will provide a sustained supply of energy throughout your walk.

Familiarisation

Study your map and familiarise yourself with the route and various landmarks, where possible visit the areas before you walk. An escape route should be planned in case of bad weather or in the event of an emergency (see bad visibility descents).

Note where the mountain rescue posts are situated, along with the nearest telephones and areas where shelter can be provided. Look for danger areas e.g. gullies, ledges etc.

Equipment

It never ceases to surprise me how many people ascend the mountains in inappropriate clothing and footwear. People walk in jeans and T-shirts without any protection from the biting cold wind and possibly rain on the summit. Trainers are often worn to walk over the snow on Ben Nevis and the wet and muddy sections on all 3 peaks. I have witnessed a lady ascending Ben Nevis in stiletto heels and jeans/T-shirt. It is for this reason that I have included the following short list of recommendations for the inexperienced to follow.

Photo 4. View of the Ben Nevis Inn on the left at Achintee and showing the path leading off to the right

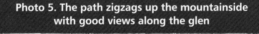

Photo 5. The path zigzags up the mountainside with good views along the glen

Boots

These are an essential item on this walk. A good fitting pair of walking boots can make the difference between success or failure on any walk. Ankle protection is important especially on the peaks of Ben Nevis and Scafell Pike (photo 23), where large stones and scree can inflict damage very easily.

Before buying boots always try them on wearing the socks you will use with them. The boots should not be too tight as to cramp your toes, likewise not too slack that your feet move around inside.

Socks

These should keep the feet warm and cushion them from any knocks and constant pounding. You can usually buy short, medium or long and thick/thin depending on preference. Take several pairs as a clean pair of socks gives feet a new lease of life.

Trousers

Should be loose fitting and ideally made of cotton or a fleece type of material. Cotton trousers will be light to wear, keep you warm and most importantly will dry quickly when wet.

Jeans are not suitable for walking as they take a long time to dry when wet and become very heavy. They can also chafe the skin and draw the body heat, so giving you hypothermia, and their insulating property is very low.

Hat/gloves

Much of the body's heat is lost through the head, so hat and gloves are strongly recommended.

Jacket/waterproof trousers

There is a vast assortment of jackets available for this type of venture from fleece to coated breathable materials. If there is a hood attached this will give good protection around the head. Whichever jacket you are buying, ensure it is waterproof and not just shower proof.

Waterproof trousers are necessary to keep you dry on those wet days. Do not wear water/wind proofs any longer than necessary as quite often condensation builds up inside.

Breathable Clothing

Clothing which is classed as breathable is only breathable as long as the pores of the item are not blocked, e.g. when wet!

Rucksack

This should be large enough to hold all your personal and safety equipment. Put a liner inside to keep your clothes and other items dry in very wet conditions. Use the rucksack pockets to put small or frequently needed items in, i.e. water bottle, map, food etc.

Clothing

Clothing should be built up in layers where warm air can be trapped between each layer. Three thin tops or T-shirts are more effective than one thick one. If you are hot you can easily take a layer off.

EMERGENCY EQUIPMENT

Torch

Each person should carry one; take spare batteries and a bulb. Check it works before each mountain.

Pencil & Notebook

It may be necessary to take notes on route especially in an emergency when positions, names, injuries etc. should be written and passed on to emergency services.

Whistle

Each person should carry a plastic whistle (metal ones can freeze in the cold) and they should also be familiar with the 'S.O.S.' signal to alert others in times of emergency.

Survival Bag

Designed for a walker to get inside to protect them from the harsh environment and to preserve body heat. It is a piece of safety equipment that may never be used but should always be carried.

Photo 6. One of the two bridges taking you across a burn before the path ascends steeply around Meall an t-Suidhe

EQUIPMENT SELECTION

When considering equipment and clothing for this walk, you must remember that it may be a calm, still, and what seems like a nice day in Glen Nevis but nearing the summit of any mountain it can be cold and very windy with low cloud. Often it is the wind chill factor that causes problems for walkers. With this in mind, the following suggested list of items should help you to both complete the walk and stay warm, dry and hopefully injury free.

EQUIPMENT CHECKLIST

- ❑ Compass and guide book
- ❑ Walking boots
- ❑ Walking socks including 2 spare sets
- ❑ Walking trousers (no jeans)
- ❑ Warm upper body clothing (in layers)
- ❑ Spare clothing
- ❑ Gloves, hat
- ❑ Torch with spare bulb and batteries
- ❑ Whistle
- ❑ Note paper and pencil
- ❑ Toilet paper
- ❑ Survival bag
- ❑ Basic first aid kit including plasters and Vaseline
- ❑ Fleece/waterproof fabric outer jacket/cagoule
- ❑ Over trousers, waterproof
- ❑ Day rucksack
- ❑ Food/drinks
- ❑ Camera
- ❑ Maps of the three relevant areas.
- ❑ Gaiters – optional
- ❑ Watch

Other items you may wish to take

Sun cream, midge repellent, mobile phone and sun hat

Use this as a checklist before you leave home.

THE BODY

Should be kept warm. Build clothes up in layers with wind/waterproofs on top.

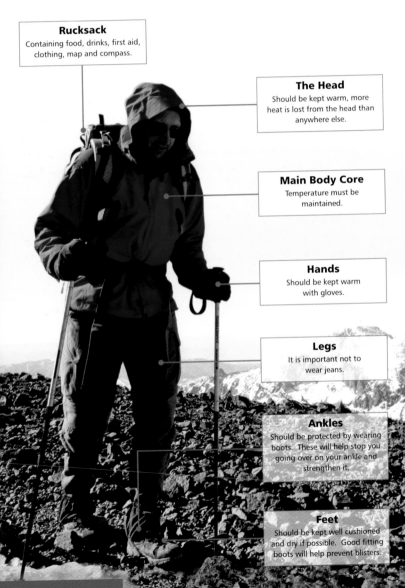

Rucksack
Containing food, drinks, first aid, clothing, map and compass.

The Head
Should be kept warm, more heat is lost from the head than anywhere else.

Main Body Core
Temperature must be maintained.

Hands
Should be kept warm with gloves.

Legs
It is important not to wear jeans.

Ankles
Should be protected by wearing boots. These will help stop you going over on your ankle and strengthen it.

Feet
Should be kept well cushioned and dry if possible. Good fitting boots will help prevent blisters.

BOOTS & BLISTERS

Two of the most important things on this walk are your feet and boots. If your feet hurt or you suffer with bad blisters, then you may not complete the walk. Boots need to be big enough to fit comfortably but not too big so your feet move around inside whilst walking. Remember to fit the boots with the socks you will be wearing, when buying.

Sprinkle a liberal quantity of talcum powder on your feet and in the socks. Put talcum powder into your boots and on the outside of your socks, then put your boots on making sure your feet fit snugly into them. This method has helped many people to keep their feet not only dry and fresh throughout but more importantly blister free after 25 miles.

Change socks as often as you feel you need to. Doing this will refresh your feet and provide cushioning. If you feel any warm spots on your feet or toes, do not wait until a blister has formed, it is too late then. Change socks, sprinkle foot powder on or put a plaster on.

Remember to cut your toenails short before you leave home so you don't get any undue pressure on your toes whilst walking or descending the mountains, which will result in black and painful toenails or the loss of them!

FIRST AID

Knowledge of basic first aid would be helpful on any walk. To be able to bandage cracked ribs, put a sling on or dress a wound can be vital in times of accidents, especially on the higher crags, when hypothermia can set in.

In any accident or emergency situation the ability to reassure the casualty and comfort them is very important, do not move the casualty if the accident is of a possible serious nature e.g. a back or head injury. Keep the casualty warm and reassured then send for help. Someone should stay with the injured person. If the injury is not of a serious nature the injured person should, if and when possible, be removed from danger.

The possibility of shock or delayed shock can present further problems for the casualty, so reassurance and company is vital. The majority of accidents happen on the return or second half of the journey, probably due to fatigue, cold, tiredness or complacency. Be aware and alert throughout the walk to possible dangers.

Common Types of Injuries

- *Cuts and grazes*
- *Blisters*
- *Hypothermia*
- *Sprained Ankle/Wrist*
- *Broken Arms/Legs*
- *Cracked Ribs*
- *Head Injuries*
- *Gashed Shins*
- *Toe nails dropping off – cut before you go!*

All the above, can prove fatal, especially on an exposed area of the mountain or in times of panic, fog or adverse conditions.

Individual First Aid Kit

- *Adhesive Dressing*
- *Triangular Bandage*
- *Bandage*
- *Safety Pins*
- *Waterproof Container*
- *Sterile Dressing*
- *Crepe Bandage*
- *Gauze/Lint*
- *Scissors*
- *Micropore*
- *Sun Cream*
- *Insect Repellent*

HYPOTHERMIA

Hypothermia is caused when the body core temperature falls below 35°C. If a walker is not properly prepared for the conditions or the clothing worn is not satisfactory, then a combination of the cold, wet, exhaustion and the wind chill factor can give a walker hypothermia.

When you stop walking for a while, you quickly get cold. To combat this, put another layer on, zip up and put gloves and hat on.

The Signs and Symptoms in Descending Order: -

- *Shivering*
- *Cold, pale and dry skin*
- *Low body temperature*
- *Irrational behaviour*
- *A gradual slip into unconsciousness*
- *Pulse and respiratory rate slow*
- *Difficulty in detecting breathing and pulse when unconscious*
- *Death*

Ways of Preventing Hypothermia

- Build up body clothing in thin layers, adding on or taking off as necessary.
- Have suitable wind/waterproofs with you.
- Take some food/hot drink or boiled sweets, which produce energy and heat during digestion.
- Wear a balaclava/woolly hat to insulate the head, and some gloves.
- Shelter out of the wind.
- Take a survival bag and if conditions dictate, use it.

In any type of emergency/accident situation it is always advisable to come off the higher ground as soon as possible especially in low cloud, snow or other bad conditions. The temperature difference between a valley and the high ground can be several degrees.

Treatment for Hypothermia

- Provide extra clothing and shelter from the elements.
- Bodily warmth of others helps in a gradual warming.
- If well enough come down into a warmer sheltered area.
- Give hot drinks if conscious.
- Give chocolate or sweets if the patient can still take food.
- The casualty should be placed so that the head is slightly lower than the body.

DO NOT *rub the skin or use a hot water bottle as this can cause a surge of blood from the central body core to the surface, this could prove fatal.*

Alcohol should not be consumed on any walk and should not be given to anyone who has hypothermia. The body temperature will be lowered as well as giving a false sense of security.

Photo 7. The steps are often steep and uneven throughout

TOP TIPS FOR COMPLETING THE 3 PEAKS

- Prepare and train before the walk. Those who do some training and preparation usually succeed, those who do not, don't succeed.

- Take and wear the right walking clothing. This includes boots, waterproof jacket and trousers (see equipment list). No jeans, T-shirt or high heels!

- Carry at least two spare pairs of walking socks and change them if you need to. This will help to revive your feet and give them new life.

- Eat little and often. Doing this will give a constant supply and release of energy to the body.

- Drink regularly. If the body becomes dehydrated, you will lose energy fast.

- Carry a map and compass with you and know how to use them. Ensure you have emergency and first aid items with you including torch, whistle, survival bag, first aid kit and blister plasters.

- If you feel a blister forming or a warm spot on your feet, do not wait until the blister has formed before you do something about it. Stop and put a plaster on before it is too late. Look after your feet and they will look after you!

- Cut toenails short before you leave home.

- Carry only items you need for ascending each mountain and no more. Remember you have to walk up and down the 3 highest mountains in the UK. Grams turn into kilograms, ounces into pounds every time you put something more into your rucksack.

- Leave details of your route and approximate return time with the support team/B&B/friends.

- If walking at night, ensure you carry spare batteries and bulb. Do not be left in darkness.

- On reaching the summit, only stay as long as necessary. If you feel cold then leave the summit and descend to lower ground where it is usually warmer and more sheltered.

MOUNTAIN SAFETY

Details of your route should be left with your support team or someone who can monitor your progress and most importantly alert the rescue services if you are overdue. Because you plan a route it does not mean you have to use it. It is better to cancel if there is a problem than to risk lives ascending a mountain in atrocious conditions or badly prepared.

Many people do not realise that a calm sunny day in the valley can mean low cloud and gale force winds on the summit, add to this the wind chill factor and a walker badly prepared has got problems. Bad weather can sweep in quickly. It is usually warmer and better weather on lower ground, so if cold but uninjured, make your way to the lower ground if you encounter problems while walking.

Only walk routes which are within the capability of your party. One of the most common problems that can lead to accidents is walkers becoming separated from each other. There should be a party leader and that person should ensure the group walks at a sensible pace. This is usually the speed of the slowest walker. Each person should carry a map and compass and a route card and they should all have been involved in drawing up the route before hand. See, copy and use the sample route card inside back cover.

If you are delayed e.g. you have descended into the wrong valley, inform your base or the police as quickly as possible to avoid the mountain rescue team from being called out unnecessarily.

All walkers should be familiar with the
INTERNATIONAL DISTRESS SIGNAL
- 6 long blasts on whistle
- 6 shouts or waves of handkerchief
- 6 flashes of torch in succession

All followed by a pause of one minute, then repeated.
A red flare is a distress signal.

Photo 8. The path ascends steeply near the burn as you head towards Lochan Meall an t-Suidhe

THE COUNTRY CODE

- Be safe, plan ahead and follow any signs.
- Leave gates and property as you find them.
- Protect plants and animals and take your litter home including any glass.
- Keep dogs under close control.
- Consider other people, especially if you are passing through villages at night on route. Keep noise to a minimum.
- Guard against all risk of fire.
- Be conscious of footpath erosion at all times.
- Don't touch livestock, machinery or crops.
- Use gates and stiles to cross walls and fences.
- Leave nothing but footprints, take nothing but photographs

WEATHER FORECASTS

The importance of checking the weather reports before you ascend each peak can be vital to the success or failure of your team.

Notices displaying the current weather patterns on the peaks of Ben Nevis and Snowdon are usually near the start of the routes described. It is advisable to listen to the forecast on local radio if possible for the area you are in.

Calm, still weather in the valley or glen can turn to gale force winds on the peaks. Check your forecast before you ascend, are you liable to encounter low cloud, heavy rain, snow or scorching sun on your journey? Usually the forecast can help in deciding what time to start walking and what type and how much extra clothing you need to take with you and whether you need sun cream, insect repellent and extra fluid.

Photo 9. View showing a large part of the first half of the route with the Lochan situated behind the mountain and Glen Nevis in the foreground

When walking in mountainous country you can often tell if there is or will be deterioration in the weather by the onset of low cloud around the peaks. Before this happens check your present position and look in the direction you are intending to go as far as you can see. Take a bearing with your compass then follow that bearing through the cloud to your intended destination using both map and compass where necessary. Never be caught unawares, when you reach that spot look again as far as you can see, take your bearing again then proceed as before.

On the National 3 Peaks snow can present problems at certain times of the year. 'Driving' snow creates whiteout conditions. Where conditions are very bad (photo 27), then only those with a great amount of experience should be on the mountains. In virtually every type of situation like this it may be better to abandon the attempt than to risk lives on dangerous peaks.

Photo 10. The path with Lochan Meall an t-Suidhe just off to the left. This point is around 600m

NAVIGATION

The ability to find your way from one place to another especially in bad weather is something that needs to be learned. Although we may have a sixth sense or sense of direction, when the cloud is low, even the best of us can get lost quickly.

Before embarking on your 3 peaks walk you should have an understanding of the basic principles of map reading and compass use. It is not intended that this walking guide should give you the information on how to use navigational equipment but only to point out the need for walkers to be prepared before venturing out especially in bad visibility.

Learning how to read the contours of a map can be of benefit and being able to recognise landmarks seen on the map. Combined with this, basic course plotting and magnetic variation should at least help you to come down from the mountain in any problem situation.

There is a need to practice your navigation skills until you feel confident enough to venture onto the hills and moorland. Most people know the general principles of pilotage where the sun rises in the east and sets in the west, you can therefore get some idea on a clear day as to which general direction you are walking in, however you would not know if you were heading into danger e.g. steep gullies, cliffs or overhangs.

There are many books that deal with map and compass training and courses are available to those that seek them. Use and learn as much as possible about map and compass work.

Over recent years the use of hand held GPS systems has become much more widespread. They are very useful for pinpointing your position, particularly in bad weather. I strongly recommend them. If taking one on your 3 peaks venture, take some spare batteries.

GRID REFERENCES

You may find it necessary at some time to either find a place from a given grid reference or to make a grid reference from a place on a map.

All maps have grid lines running north/south and east/west. These are called 'Eastings' and 'Northings' and these lines have numbers on them. They can be further split into tenths, the numbers range from 00 to 99.

Grid references are normally given in six figures. The first three figures indicate how far to the east the place is. The second three figures indicate how far to the north the place is.

To make a grid reference look from left to right on a map. Read the numbers going from left to right, write the numbers for the grid line to the left of your position, estimate the tenths to your position and write that number down to make 3 numbers.

Now look up your map and write the 2 numbers from the line just below your position. Repeat the second sequence as above. You should now have 6 numbers usually written as GR. 647556

In using this method you should be able to pinpoint your target or position quite accurately on a 1:25000 scale map. Before you ascend the peaks you need to practise until you can both find grid reference points on a map and create a grid reference from a given position e.g. the grid reference for Ben Nevis is 167713 at the 'trig' point, using 6 figures, and on O.S. Explorer map 392 Ben Nevis & Fort William.

MAP OF WEST OF SCOTLAND

Fort William can be freely accessed from throughout the country. There are roads and rail links to Fort William as well as airports in Inverness and Glasgow (see useful telephone numbers in back of book). Fort William is situated at the southern end of the Great Glen.

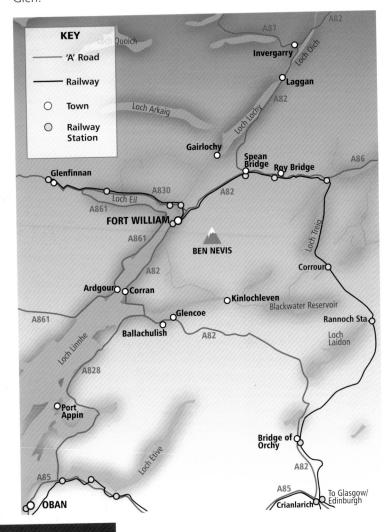

FORT WILLIAM & GLEN NEVIS AREA

Fort William is the main town near the foothills of Ben Nevis. It also represents the start or end of the Caledonian Canal, which runs to Inverness on the east coast. The West Highland Way ends here and The Great Glen Way starts here.

Within the area there are many outdoor activity centres, which cover all manner of water sports and land based activities. Fort William Tourist Information Centre provides interesting displays of local attractions as well as general information about the area.

The Glen Nevis Visitor Centre gives information, especially on Ben Nevis and Glen Nevis area.

Photo 11. Lochan Meall an t-Suidhe on the left as the stony path continues up the mountainside

Photo 12. Excellent views as you walk now on small loose stone at around 800m

The 'Ben Path' starts out relatively easy but becomes increasingly rocky, arduous and exposed. Many people do not appreciate their level of fitness and how difficult they may find it. Plan to set off early in the morning to avoid returning in the dark.

The majority of accidents happen on the return journey which can be just as tiring as the ascent. Take this into consideration when planning your ascent.

**Photo 13. The path now zigzags as the grass disappears
and you are walking on the higher slopes**

There are many mountains in the area to walk, whisky distilleries to visit, cable cars and cruises to venture on. Local restaurants around Fort William offer good food.

Many of the buildings are stone built and the town is clean and pleasant. The local people are keen to welcome visitors and there are numerous hostelries in which to sample local ale. A visit to the town is not to be missed. There are several outdoor shops selling maps, compasses and most outdoor equipment.

Loch Linnhe borders Fort William and provides fishing and sailing for those who enjoy alternative sports and hobbies. Those walkers who have time to relax after climbing Ben Nevis will find the area around Fort William very pleasant and picturesque. A wide range of shops cater for all tastes in local food and souvenirs. Over recent years the area has become a film set with films like Braveheart, Harry Potter and Highlander being filmed here.

Travelling to Fort William by car will give some of the best views anywhere in the U.K. particularly travelling through Glen Coe. A rail and bus link will also transport you there from throughout the British Isles. Take a camera to give you some lasting memories.

The path to the summit of Ben Nevis (photo 5), was originally built as a pony track to service the observatory and the hotel on the summit, which are now in ruins. The observatory was operational between 1883-1904. During the summers of 1881-82, Clement Wragge climbed to the summit each day to record daily temperatures. The average temperature between 1884 to 1903 was only 0.3°C.

A 4-bedroom hotel was built close to the weather station by a Mr. White and run by two ladies during the summer months. It did not stay open for many years however, and the ruins can be seen on the summit today.

Surprisingly there have been a number of cars that have actually driven to the summit. In 1911, Henry Alexander was the first man to the top in a 20 horsepower Ford model T. Since then there have been several cars that have reached the summit. The fastest was 7 hours 23 minutes in 1928 by George Simpson in an Austin 7.

Dudley Grierson from London went up on a motorbike in 1901. Since then there have been various ascents using horse and carts, beds, wheelbarrows and carrying items like barrels of beer and pedal organs.

The highest war memorial in Britain is situated on this summit. The views from here are breathtaking in all directions.

The tourist path is used for the Ben Nevis annual race, which takes place on the first Saturday in September. It takes around 2 hours for the fittest to complete the 14 miles from the start to the summit and back. The Lochaber mountain rescue team supervise this.

The road along Glen Nevis runs for approximately 7 miles. You will find the Visitor Centre, the Glen Nevis Caravan & Camping Park and the Glen Nevis Youth Hostel along this road. The mountains tower on both sides of the glen where the road eventually stops at a car park at the far end.

Photo 14. View of Loch Linnhe as you reach the final section of the path to the summit

BEN NEVIS

Summit
1344m

Five Finger Gully

▲
To North Face

Red Burn

B
Youth Hostel

Ben Nevis Inn
Achintee

P

A
P

Glen Nevis Visitor Centre
(Only public toilets in Glen Nevis)

GLEN NEVIS

BEN NEVIS GRID REFERENCES

Many people have GPS systems, so to assist those people, here are a list of GPS grid references so you can pre-enter the co-ordinates before you leave home.

The route is from the Visitor Centre in Glen Nevis to the summit walking on the popular mountain track. On your way up the path, when you reach the area near the Lochan, at GR.147724, ensure you follow the mountain track and not the path to the north face.

The route is both undulating and winding so allowance must be made for this when walking and using the GPS in low visibility.

Map to use is O.S. Explorer NO.392 Ben Nevis & Fort William.

Start Glen Nevis Visitor Centre

GR. 123730

GR. 123732

GR. 126728

GR. 131723

GR. 140718

GR. 147724 Lochan (turn right on path)

GR. 147718

GR. 147715

GR. 149717

GR. 151713

GR. 155715

GR. 157715

GR. 161713

GR. 166712

GR. 167713 'Trig' Point

WALKING ROUTE - BEN NEVIS

There are 2 main starting points to climb Ben Nevis:
- Glen Nevis Visitor Centre (recommended).
- The Youth Hostel

START A - GLEN NEVIS VISITOR CENTRE (RECOMMENDED)

Start by touching the water of Loch Linnhe beside Crannog Sea Food Restaurant, near the main car park in Fort William. It is also the main ferry terminal. Take the Inverness road then at the sign to Glen Nevis at the Nevis Bridge roundabout go straight across. From the roundabout it is 1.2 miles to the Glen Nevis Visitor Centre (photo1). **Park in the free car park here**. Near the car park is a pedestrian suspension bridge crossing the River Nevis. A sign points to Ben Path. Follow this passing a guesthouse. The visitor centre is now opposite.

Photo 15. The summit of Ben Nevis with the 'trig' point, emergency shelter and ruins of the observatory and hotel

A sign states 'Ben Path' (photo 3) ascend for 150m following the main path and signs. As you ascend you have a good view of Glen Nevis Caravan & Camping Park to your right. The path becomes stony, uneven and ascends steeply. Continue on this path, which eventually joins path 'B'.

START B - YOUTH HOSTEL

Start by touching the water as 'A'. Take the Inverness road, a sign at the Nevis Bridge roundabout points across to Glen Nevis. Pass Glen Nevis Caravan and Camping Park and park opposite the youth hostel 370m further along the road (limited parking). This is 2.1 miles from the roundabout. Do not park in Glen Nevis Caravan Park or use their facilities unless you are staying there.

Your ascent of Ben Nevis begins here. Immediately opposite the youth hostel there is a footbridge, cross it, then cross some steps over a fence. A sign here (photo 2), usually displays a description of Ben Nevis with the current weather forecast and other information.

Continue steeply up a winding, stony path, a man made path develops forming steps as you ascend. Part way up, the path joins path 'A'.

Both paths converge (photo 9), and you cross over a wooden platform bridge. You are now on the main path ascending Ben Nevis, which is known as 'The mountain track'. The path is very stony and more uneven on this section. Approximately 80m further up is a seat on a bend in the path. You come to a metal bridge and this point affords good views of Glen Nevis (Front Cover).

Cross over a small burn running down a gully, the path here is hard mud, interspersed with stones as it winds up the hillside. The path turns sharp left then right, followed by steps up a steep rock outcrop. The sound of a fast flowing burn running down another gully can be heard. A natural spring escapes from the hillside so the path is usually wet here.

A stone outcrop and another metal bridge (photo 6) with a waterfall beneath is crossed. The path then ascends steeply between the two mountains with Red Burn on your right. While ascending the side of the mountain burn you come to a sign saying Conservation Area. The path twists left and right (photo 8), as you approach the loch halfway up the mountain (photo 11). The path levels out a little here (photo 10), as you walk on a recently made stone path. The area is open with a large expanse of grass. Lochan Meall an t-Suidhe is on the left.

Follow the path as it turns immediately right and uphill again by a section of wall and some piles of stones at the bend in the path. It is important to note that the path going straight on leads to the area climbers use.

Cross a small stream which runs down the path. There are good views across the mountains. To your right there are some steep drops off. Cross another burn where walkers often stop for refreshment. Approaching the upper slopes, you can look down the glen to the youth hostel. Stay on the main path towards the summit.

The final zigzag ascent (photo 13) is very rocky and uneven, with loose stone and scree (photo 12). **The top of the five finger gully has a deceptive gentle slope (see sketch, page 44) which quickly leads to dangerous cliffs. Pay attention and ensure you are heading in the right direction**. As you approach the gully the route bends sharp right on the scree path. Near the summit the path levels out, with a lot of small stones. Quite often, up to mid summer, the area is covered in snow.

You may see small piles of stones on your ascent as you proceed if there is no snow (photo 14). Follow your path carefully and if there is snow, it is important to stay on the path.

Immediately before the summit take extreme care of the sheer drops over the edge of the mountain, down the infamous Gardyloo Gully, Tower Gully and No.2 Gully. Stay on the path watching for snow overhangs, which can be deceiving. The gully just before the flat plateau summit is close to the path, so keep right, heading for the ruins of the observatory, which dates back to Victorian Times. On reaching the summit (photo 15, 16) you have excellent views in all directions (cloud permitting). There is a triangulation pillar, number S1595 and emergency shelter. A cross with a cairn and plaque states it is Britain's highest War Memorial. It is the Fort William Dudley/Worcestershire Cairn of Remembrance.

After resting for a short time on the summit you may find the cold penetrating the body. This is now the time to start your descent to warmer and more sheltered areas. Retrace your steps down the mountain ensuring you return on the correct path.

In times of bad visibility follow the bearings and directions given in the chapter on bad visibility descents. **N.B.** Ben Nevis should be treated with respect at all times, at over 4,000ft the weather on top can be very different to what you expect e.g. deep snow in May and thick fog and ice. You must carry good quality maps of Ben Nevis with bad visibility routes in scales of 1:10,000 or better. This is for your safety and that of others.

Photo 16. View to the southeast from the summit of Ben Nevis with the clouds below

DRIVING ROUTE TO SCAFELL PIKE

	ROAD	DESTINATION
Leave Fort William	**A82**	North Ballachulish
at North Ballachulish	**A82**	Crianlarich via Rannoch Moor
at Crainlarich	**A82**	Tarbet
at Tarbet	**A82**	Dumbarton
at Dumbarton	**A82**	Erskine Toll Bridge
at Erskine Toll Bridge	**M898**	Glasgow
at Bridge (south)	**M8**	M74
on M74	**M74**	Abington
at Abington	**A74M**	Gretna
at Gretna	**M74/M6**	Carlisle
*at Carlisle	**M6**	Penrith
at Penrith	**A66**	Keswick
at Keswick	**B5289**	Grange
at Grange	**B5289**	Seatoller
at Seatoller	**Minor**	Seathwaite

Leave Walkers - Drive to Wasdale Head for pick-up - Optional

at Seathwaite	**B5289**	Crummock Water
at Crummock Water	**B5289**	Brackenthwaite
at Brackenthwaite	**Minor**	Mockerkin Tarn A5086
at Mockerkin Tarn	**A5086**	Egremont
at Egremont	**A595**	Gosforth
at Gosforth	**Minor**	Wellington
at Wellington	**Minor**	Wastwater
at Wastwater	**Minor**	Wasdale Head

Route from Carlisle direct to Wastwater - Recommended

*at Carlisle	**A595**	Cockermouth
near Cockermouth	**A5086**	Egremont
at Egremont	**A595**	Gosforth

At Gosforth turn left onto minor roads to Wasdale Head. Park in car park on left opposite the packhorse bridge, just past the northern end of Wastwater or turn right over the bridge into the National Trust car park at the side of the campsite (charge).

SCAFELL AREA

Wastwater on the southwestern side of the Lake District and Derwent Water to the north borders Scafell Pike. The nearest main towns of Keswick and Ambleside are within easy reach by car.

There are numerous small villages all round the area with the occasional shop or public house. Picnic areas abound throughout the Lake District especially around the lakes themselves. Birds and other wildlife are plentiful. Scafell Pike is in the heart of the largest national park in England, which has 16 lakes within its area. The National Trust owns much of the area.

When ascending Scafell Pike from Seathwaite via the Corridor Route, ample parking can be found in Seathwaite. You arrive there by passing Grange at the southern end of Derwent Water. There is a café at Seathwaite and a trout farm.

Photo 17. The start at Wasdale Head with Scafell Pike in the background. The route is along the valley.

Approaching Scafell foothills from Wastwater there is a small car park on the left and a large National Trust car park (charge) over the small bridge on your right beside a campsite together at the northern end of the lake. Here is the start of the walk. Continuing up the road to where it ends one mile further on past the end of the lake you will find Wasdale Head Hotel. Next to it is an outdoor shop, which has a small campsite opposite it. All around here is mountainous with spectacular scenery.

On the final approach to the summit of Scafell Pike you will see Great Gable with Sty Head Tarn below and Derwent Water in the distance. This is the general direction of the Corridor Route. Looking the opposite way you see Wastwater back down in the valley. During darkness on moonlit nights, you can often see Wastwater and its reflection. This will give you an unmistakable point to aim for on your descent during darkness. Take care to pick out your path carefully on a night descent. The route from Wasdale up to the summit during darkness is by far the easiest to walk and navigate, but leaving the summit in darkness or low cloud and descending off the pike its self can be a lot more difficult.

In times of low cloud you should navigate carefully to get off the summit to lower ground as this can prove testing for walkers.

The first sections of the walk from Seathwaite via the Corridor Route to the summit are good but it becomes progressively more difficult as you proceed.

Whichever route you choose pick out your path carefully, use your map and compass wisely and accurately.

Take your waterproofs with you when visiting Seathwaite. This was once **the wettest place in Great Britain**, now superseded by Fort William!

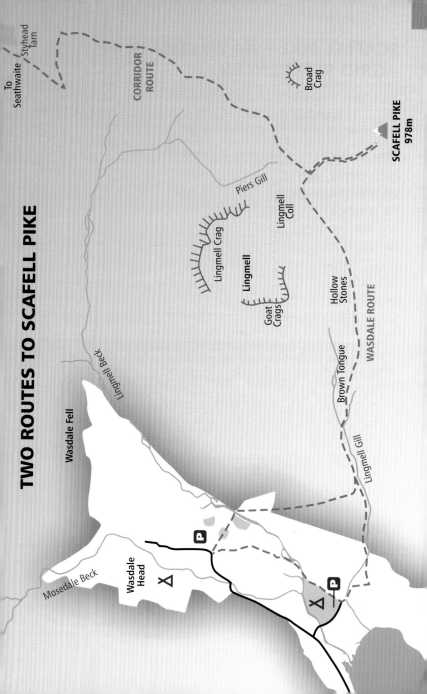

TWO ROUTES TO SCAFELL PIKE

To Seathwaite

Styhead Tarn

CORRIDOR ROUTE

Broad Crag

SCAFELL PIKE 978m

Piers Gill

Lingmell Crag

Lingmell Coll

Lingmell

Goat Crags

Hollow Stones

WASDALE ROUTE

Brown Tongue

Wasdale Fell

Lingmell Beck

Lingmell Gill

Mosedale Beck

Wasdale Head

SCAFELL PIKE - via Wasdale Head – GRID REFERENCES

Starting at the car park on the minor road opposite the bridge: -
The route is undulating and winding so allowance must be made
for this when walking and using the GPS.

Map to use is O.S. OL6 Lakes South-western area.

GR. 180076 Start
GR. 186072 Footbridge
GR. 193074
GR. 195074 Brown Tongue
GR. 205074
GR. 212078
GR. 215076
GR. 217074
GR. 215072 'Trig' point

**Photo 18. Passing the cottage on the way up the valley.
Note the waymarker denoting the path**

WALKING ROUTES - SCAFELL PIKE
- via Wasdale Head

Approach on the undulating road alongside Wastwater. A sign points to Wasdale Head. Turn right over the stone packhorse bridge. A car park (charge) is at the side of the campsite at the end of Wastwater. Your ascent of Scafell Pike begins here. A compass bearing from the car park looking directly to Scafell Pike is 98°M.

Turn left out of the car park and walk up the stony farmers track. Cross over a cattle grid (photo 17), then cross a bridge where the beck flows into Wastwater 100m to the right. Turn left where a small wooden sign points to Eskdale, then up the right side of the beck.

Near a cottage (photo 18), another small sign says 'Permissive Path, Scafell' which passes the left side of the house.

About 100m past the house there is a footbridge, which crosses the small stream. Cross, then go through a gate, follow the path ascending to the right.

A sign states 'National Trust Property' and is next to a kissing gate. Go through onto a narrow path, this is stony in places, winding its way up the mountain between the bracken on your left and the stream on your right. The path ascends steeply in places and numerous large rocks cover the path.

Looking back you can see Wastwater and the Irish Sea in the background beyond Workington Power Station. Scafell Pike is the sheer cliffs you can see directly ahead at the top of the valley. Pass through another kissing gate with the beck still on the right. Continue up the very stony path.

A compass bearing taken just before Brown Tongue and in direct line to the Pike reads 98°M. You now come to a section of man made cobbled path, which is easier to walk on. You can now see Brown Tongue and here is another section of cobbled path with a pile of stones formed into a cairn.

You now cross the beck at the foot of Brown Tongue (photo19), where you will see the path across the far side of the beck. Ascend the cobbled path alongside another beck (photo 20).

A small cairn marks a fork in the path; take the left path into heather and peat. The path turns stony soon after. You can see the path ahead but in parts it is not so well defined. The ground is flatter here with grass and lots of stones scattered around (photo 21).

There is a scree slope leading to Mickledore to the right between the Pike and Scafell itself. It is a shorter route to the top but more dangerous to ascend or descend the scree slope, especially at night.

Small cairns mark the main path which is small stone and shale with grass on both sides. There is a stone outcrop to the left side of the Pike. Skirt around the left side of it (photo 22), look for small cairns. Walk in a semi-circle to the large stone outcrop ahead, then look carefully to the right for the piles of stones on the final ascent to the Pike.

Much of the remaining section consists of large stones, which you must walk over (photo 23). One slip and you could break an ankle between the stones, so take care here. Look to your left as you ascend, you should see Sty Head Tarn, which is near to the beginning of the Corridor Route to Scafell Pike from Seathwaite. Beyond this tarn is Derwent Water.

On gaining the summit there is a triangulation pillar and a wind shelter. Views from the summit include the Scottish Borders, Blackpool, and Windermere and on a clear night the lights of Douglas on the Isle of Man can be seen.

On this, as on any mountain peak, it can be very cold with gale force winds. The wind chill factor should be taken seriously, so windproof clothing needs to be worn before reaching the summit.

On the return journey down the mountain pick out the path carefully especially in the dark. In the event of low cloud or loss of bearings on the summit, follow the bad visibility descent detailed in this book. On a dark but moonlit night the reflection of Wastwater is usually very evident and should help to point you in the general direction of Wasdale Head.

Photo 19. Crossing Lingmell Gill at Brown Tongue with Scafell Pike in the background

WALKING ROUTES SCAFELL PIKE
- via Seathwaite, (Corridor Route)

When you arrive at Seathwaite there is parking available along the minor road before the farm. Nearby are a small café and a trout farm. Your ascent via the Corridor Route to Scafell Pike starts here.

As you start walking you go through a farm gate, continue on the path. Follow the path to a stile and gate, continue on the path into the distance going up the valley. Cross a small wooden bridge over the river. The path starts to ascend as you go up into the head of the valley. Following the course of the stream you come to a gate and stile. The path is undulating.

Cross the small but impressive stone packhorse bridge ahead. When you pass through the gate nearby, the path starts to ascend steeply. Go through a small gate between a stone wall, the obvious path bears off to the right.

Looking back at night towards Seathwaite you can often see a small light at the farm. This is a guide for any walkers returning at night by this route, especially in bad weather.

Approaching the head of the valley the path flattens a little. A waterfall runs on your right and the path becomes very uneven and turns slightly left between the head of the two hills. It is very important to keep the beck on your right because in extreme weather conditions there is a tendency to walk to the higher ground on the left then cross the beck onto the right side which is damp and boggy.

The path along by the beck is very uneven with large stones and is difficult to walk over. There is a cairn on the level area between the two hills. It may be surrounded by water in extreme conditions but is a good route marker. The cairn is approximately 80m from the wooden bridge you see ahead, following the rough uneven path.

Cross the bridge and the path is now on the right of the beck. In bad conditions it can be very wet. Walk up between the hills to another cairn on your left. Just past it cross the beck again still following the main path. There is a tarn on your left side called Sty Head Tarn. Cross over another beck, the path is now better to walk on.

The path starts to divide nearing the head of the valley. It is important to head for the large rocks you see ahead. The path in parts here is grass. You come to a mountain rescue first aid stretcher box.

To this point the paths are reasonably obvious to see and follow but from here the path becomes difficult to see, walk along and navigate to Scafell Pike. Take great care and constantly refer to map and compass.

Past the big stone you bear left descending slightly and cross over some marshy ground. You then rise up again over a grass area then drop down to the foot of the mountain, which is straight in front of you. A magnetic bearing of 150°M from the stretcher box should take you across and up the side of the mountain along the Corridor Route.

Pick up a distinct path up the hillside, which is very steep in places with a drop off to your right. Looking down the valley you can see Wastwater. The path winds its way to the summit and just before the path leads down and around to the left where there is a small cairn. The area is extremely steep and **CARE** should be taken. Go around the side of the waterfall known as Piers Gill. You pass another small cairn and some large rocks, which you walk between as you near the summit.

On the path there is a ravine with a waterfall. You need to be careful where you are stepping. There is another distinct waterfall coming over the edge on the right with a steep drop down. Keep in to the left side of the path.

You emerge at the foot of Scafell Pike at the base of Lingmell Col. The remaining section is large stones to walk over. Take care not to loose your footing, look for piles of stones marking the route to the summit.

It is left to you the reader to decide which route to choose. I prefer to walk up and return on the Wasdale/Wastwater route. This route is probably better for those who are not extremely skilled in map reading and using a compass. The Corridor Route is not recommended at night and especially in bad conditions. Once on the summit, if conditions are bad, follow the bad visibility descent detailed in this book.

Photo 20. Heading towards Scafell Pike as you ascend by the beck towards Hollow Stones

Photo 21. Crossing Hollow Stones approaching Scafell Pike

Photo 22. The last section up to the pike

Photo 23. The final stony ascent to the summit of Scafell Pike

DRIVING ROUTE TO SNOWDON

	ROAD	DESTINATION
Leave Car Park	Minor	Santon Bridge
at Santon Bridge	Minor	Holmrook
at Holmrook	A595	Broughton in Furness
at Broughton	A5092	Haverthwaite
at Haverthwaite	A590	J36 of M6
J36 of M6	M6	M56 Chester
M56	M56	Queensferry A494
at Queensferry	A55	Llandudno Junction
at Llandudno J'tion	A470	Betws-y-Coed
at Betws-y-Coed	A5	Capel Curig
at Capel Curig	A4086	Pass of Llanberis

Park in main car park at Pen-y-pass near the youth hostel (charge). The distance by road is approximately 500 miles from Fort William depending on which driving route you choose. Total drive time is about 10½ hours. It is recommended that you change drivers regularly to avoid driver fatigue. Care should be taken to observe the speed limits. It is better to reach your destination intact.

SNOWDON AREA

Mount Snowdon is situated in the Snowdonia National Park, covering an area of 840 square miles. The area around Snowdon is very mountainous, as you would imagine. The views all around the region are good and there are some picturesque villages within a short travelling distance.

The main recommended route is situated in the pass of Llan' where it meets with Pen-y-pass. There is a youth hostel here and a mountain rescue post. Near Pen-y-pass there are a number of small lakes or tarns. The largest Llyn Llydaw (photo 25), is a reservoir.

The town of Llanberis is 6 miles away on the shore of Llyn Padarn or Llanberis Lake. Along the shore of this lake is a steam railway, which is open to visitors. Probably the most famous tourist attraction in this area is the Snowdon Mountain Railway. This line starts in Llanberis and continues to the summit of Snowdon. It is Britain's only rack and pinion mountain railway.

On the summit there is a café (new in 2008) and gift shop where thirsty walkers can quench their thirst and purchase souvenirs. Some walkers prefer to travel one way on the railway and the other on foot.

Throughout the area there are many tourist attractions but to do justice to them you need to spend a number of days exploring, walking and visiting all that the Snowdon area has to offer (see section on attractions). A few miles away are Betws-y-Coed and Caernarfon, which are well worth visiting.

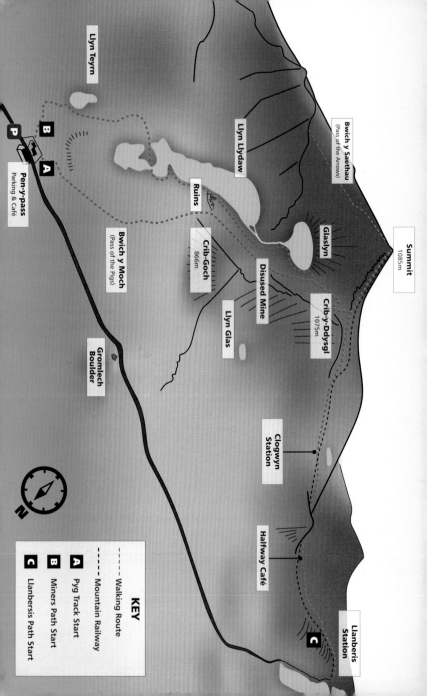

Photo 24. The car park and start of the Pyg Track at Pen-y-pass

Photo 25. Looking down from the Pyg track to the Miners Track and Llyn Llydaw Reservoir

SNOWDON GRID REFERENCES

The route is from the car park at Pen-y-pass (photo 24), on the Pyg Track which joins the Miners Track ¾ of the way to the summit (photo 26). It finishes at the 'trig' point on Snowdon summit.

The route is both undulating and winding so allowance must be made for this when walking in low visibility.

Map to use is O.S. OL17 Snowdon

Starting at Pen-y-pass car park: -

GR. 648556
GR. 644555
GR. 640554
GR. 635554
GR. 631551
GR. 625548
GR. 615549
GR. 609549
GR. 608547
GR. 610544 'Trig' point

WALKING ROUTES - SNOWDON

There are 3 main starting points to climb Snowdon on the 3 peaks walk. The Pyg Track is the easiest and most popular; the others are the Miners Track and the Llanberis Path, which ascends from the village of Llanberis.

START A - THE PYG TRACK

Park at Pen-y-pass car park opposite the youth hostel near the top of Llanberis Pass. This car park can be very busy, there is a charge for parking. Your ascent of Snowdon begins here.

Your path is in the upper right hand corner of the car park (photo 24), follow this to a stone wall with an opening between. There are good views from here down the valley. You will see the narrow slate path in front of you. The path ascends a hill, it is very uneven with slabs of stone formed into steps. You can see the obvious path winding up the mountain, keep to this undulating path.

You come to some posts and a wire fence, there are good views of Crib Goch and Llyn Llydaw Reservoir (photo 25), can be seen in the valley. As you look below, you will see the Miners Track, which is the alternative route back.

A slate-chipping path winds round Crib Goch Coll. It starts to ascend as you are walking parallel with the small reservoir, you then look into the next part of the valley as you come over the coll. There is another small tarn in view, tucked into the valley floor. The path is very evident into the next part of the valley, directly across is Snowdon.

A large expanse of stone, sloping to your left is in front of you, this can be very slippery when wet, and boots are advised. You have a good view of the second tarn in front. When you round a large expanse of rock you see the third section of this path, which is undulating.

Photo 26. The Miners Track on lower ground by Glaslyn Tarn and the Pyg Track on higher ground with the worn, joining path ascending between

Photo 27. A winter ascent here on the zigzag path just before the monolith on Snowdon ridge

There are veins of quartz in much of the rock formations, these look like snow from a distance. There are the occasional piles of stones on route. As you pass a cairn on your left, the path is again scree.

The Miners Track joins from the valley below and both continue together.

Near the head of the valley is a small pool of water some 30m wide. About 70m further up there is part of a disused quarry on your left, the path bears to the right.

The ascent now is steeper with a lot of loose stone and shale. You will see a monolith directly ahead of the zigzag route (photos 27 & 28). At the head of this section there are large stone blocks to walk up. Although still ascending, the going is a little easier. From the summit ridge (photo 28), a water pipeline at the bottom of the valley can be seen.

Photo 28. View from the ridge showing the Pyg Track on higher ground and the Miners Track which skirts around the reservoirs

The view once you attain the ridge looking towards Llanberis and in all directions is spectacular. At the monolith you turn left joining the Llanberis Path for the final ascent (photo 29). The path for the remaining distance to the summit is obvious, it runs parallel with the Snowdon Mountain Railway. As you approach you will see the new café with the triangulation pillar nearby.

You can go to the triangulation pillar for the customary photograph and viewing session (photo 30). In the café there is time to relax over a variety of food and drinks while you look out and admire the views. A souvenir shop is inside the new summit building.

You may wish to return to Pen-y-pass via the Miners Track. This route takes you initially on a steep descent, after leaving the Pyg Track (photo 26), then is virtually flat for much of the way back before becoming undulating in the last part. The return to Pen-y-pass by this route is as follows: -

Retrace your steps to the monolith, and go down the zigzag path. Just past this you should see a stone/scree descent off to your right (photo 26) by a small post, leading to Glaslyn Tarn. Follow this path to the bottom taking extreme care. Once at the bottom follow the well-made track around the reservoir passing some ruined buildings on your left. Go over the causeway (photo 25) and past another tarn. This path will take you back to Pen-y-pass.

This route is an enjoyable walk and takes approximately 1½ hours to return.

START B - THE MINERS PATH

Park at Pen-y-pass car park opposite the youth hostel near the top of Llanberis Pass. This car park can be very busy, there is a charge for parking. Your ascent of Snowdon begins here.

Your path is in the lower far corner of the car park. Go through the gate marked Miners Track and continue on the good, undulating track, which winds clockwise around the mountainside. You come to Llyn Teryn, a small lake near the track and 1km further, you come to Llyn Llydaw reservoir. A causeway cuts across it (photo 25).

Continue over the causeway and around on the track in the lower valley for a further 2km. The track ascends as you leave Llyn Llydaw, passing former houses and industrial buildings of the miners on both sides on route, and then descends again to Glaslyn Tarn. This is directly below Snowdon and is where the path now ascends to join the Pyg Track on higher ground (photo 26).

As you walk around the edge of Glaslyn, look for a worn track (photo 26), and sign on your right and steps up the steep mountainside. Ascend here, where 500m further you come to another path, which is the Pyg Track. Turn left here and continue as described in start A.

The views from this point across to Snowdon and of the valley below are very good (photo 28 shows the reservoir and both the Pyg and Miners Track clearly). Many people ascend via the Pyg Track then return via The Miners Track which is, I feel, easier to walk back on, once you have descended to the bottom. It is also safer in cold, low cloud and general bad conditions if you are walking on lower ground.

START C - LLANBERIS PATH

Park your vehicle in Llanberis (photo 30), and walk to the Royal Victoria Hotel near to the Snowdon Mountain Railway. Opposite there are a number of tourist signs. One points to Snowdon Path. Follow this along the road passing a row of houses. Cross the cattle grid at the far end and ascend the very steep metalled road to a holiday house/cafe just round a sharp bend. Continue through a metal swing gate onto a stone/shale path, still ascending steeply, to a sign pointing to Snowdon through a metal gate.

Ascend an obvious rough path. The first third ascends steeply as does the last third. This also has a lot of loose stone on it making walking difficult. The central section is on a slight ascent.

On the way up you pass under two small bridges carrying the Snowdon Mountain Railway. You may see trains throughout the summer going up and down the line. You pass a café and, for some, a welcome break. This is known as the Halfway House and is a convenient refreshment stop being approximately halfway to the summit.

Stay on the obvious path right to the summit. The top half of the route is very exposed in wet and windy weather. Nearing the summit you come to a large stone monolith on your left. This is where the Pyg Track and Miners Track join in a final ascent to the summit. Continue parallel with the railway (photo 29), to the new summit café and the 'trig' point. Retrace your steps to return to Llanberis or alternatively descend on one of the other paths.

In the event of lost bearings or low clouds on the summit of Snowdon, follow the bad visibility descent to take you to safer ground.

Now you have conquered all 3 peaks of Scotland, England and Wales you can complete your challenge by driving to Caernarfon and touching the sea.

Photo 29. Walking along Snowdon ridge with the summit in the distance

Photo 30. View from the summit looking back to the zigzag path and along the ridge with Llanberis in the background

WALKING ROUTE - SLIEVE DONARD - NORTHERN IRELAND

Start in Donard car park GR. 374305, walking from the rear of the car park stay on the right of the Glen River. Walk through Donard Wood where the path ascends for 150m to Donard Bridge.

Cross the bridge to the left side of the river and walk for 400m to the next bridge, which you cross to take you to the other side again. Continue for 400m to a third bridge and 150m past it is a stile where the open area starts. It takes approx. one hour from here to the summit.

Continue on the obvious track and cross the river where it narrows. The path ascends steeply now for 500m, with a granite causeway up to the Mourne Wall. At this point Slieve Donard comes into full view and you can follow the wall to both Slieve Donard and Slieve Commedagh.

Ascend by the wall to the summit and return by the same route. The views from the summit are spectacular and include the Scottish mountains, Isle of Man, Mountains of NW England and Snowdonia in Wales.

Even though this mountain is the smallest out of the four, it can be very cold and inhospitable on the summit so if you do intend to walk the 4th peak, ensure you go properly prepared.

SLIEVE DONARD – Useful Information

SITUATED -   In the Mourne Mountains in the east.

HEIGHT –   850 metres

GRID REF   J 357277

HOW TO GET THERE

Ferry from –   Stranraer   Tel: 0870 5707070
                    Liverpool   Tel: 08444990007

Air to –   George Best Belfast City Airport
                Web site/booking www.belfastcityairport.com

Belfast International Airport
Tel: 028 9442 2888

Bus from –   Belfast Europa Bus Station
                  Tel: 028 3026 3531

FOR FURTHER INFORMATION
Kilkeel Tourist Information
Nautilus Centre
Rooney Road
Kilkeel
N. Ireland
BT34 4AG
Tel. 028 4176 2525

Newry Tourist Information
Bagenal's Castle
Castle St
Newry
BT34 2DA
Tel. 028 3031 3170

Newcastle Tourist Information

10 – 14 Central Promenade
Newcastle
Co. Down
BT33 0AA
Tel. 028 4372 2222

B&Bs

Fir Trees,

Mrs Donnan, 16 Killowen Old Rd, Rostrevor, BT34 3AD
Tel: 028 4173 8602

Glenbeigh,

Mr. Parr, 18 Victoria Sq, Rostrevor, BT34 3EU
Tel: 028 4173 8281 / 028 4173 8025

Others may be available by contacting the T.I.C.

HEIGHTS OF SURROUNDING PEAKS

Slieve Commedagh 767m

Slieve Beg 590m

Slieve Corragh 640m

BAD VISIBILITY DESCENTS

During the ascent of any mountain care should be taken especially in bad visibility.

More accidents happen on the return journey than on the ascent. It may be difficult to pick out the path of descent in low cloud or in darkness. In situations like this follow the bearings and details below to ensure a safe descent from the summit.

BEN NEVIS

Walk from the triangulation pillar on a **grid bearing** of **225°** for **120m. Caution – Do Not Veer to the Right!**

Follow a **grid bearing** of **287°** for **60m**, which should take you clear of the plateau onto your path.

Approx. **grid bearing 280°** for **800m** follow winding path. Stay on path, **do not take bearing more than 281°**

Magnetic North is estimated at 2°20′ W of Grid North in 2009, this decreases by about ½° every four years. The compass bearing is gained by adding this difference to the grid bearing, this is known as a magnetic bearing. Refer to current O.S. map for magnetic variation.

SCAFELL PIKE

Walk from the triangulation pillar on a **grid bearing** of **315°** for **300m**. Look carefully for the path and cairns.

Walk for **200m** on **grid bearing 294°**
Walk for **200m** on **grid bearing 336°**
Then walk on **grid bearing 231°**

From this point follow the descending path round left, towards Brown Tongue.

This route takes you to the left of Dropping Crag, down to Lingmell Col and left around to Hollow Stones. In this area magnetic north is 2°44' W of Grid North in 2007. Annual change is approximately 11° east. The compass bearing is gained by adding this difference to the grid bearing. Refer to current O.S. map for magnetic variation.

Following this course from the summit should bring you off the peak and below the rocks in front of the Pike itself. From this point you can follow the path downhill to Wastwater looking for the piles of stones on route.

SNOWDON

Walk from the summit station/café on **grid bearing 347°** for **500m** following the distinct path. A railway line is on the left and a steep drop on the right. At the monolith turn right on **grid bearing 48°**. You are now on another distinct path going downhill. This path zigzags sharply. Stay on this path to descend, eventually leading back to Pen-y-pass. In extreme bad weather follow the railway line down into Llanberis.

In the event of low cloud or other problem on the top half of the route, the Miners Track will take you to the valley quicker. It starts about a third of the way down the mountain and branches off to the right. The path is steep at first but once at the bottom it is a good, virtually flat path to Pen-y-pass. A sign is situated at the Pen-y-pass end of this track giving current weather conditions.

In this area magnetic north is 2° W of grid north in 2007 annual change is approximately 11° east. The compass bearing is gained by adding the difference to the grid bearing. Refer to current O.S. map for magnetic variation.

SUPPORT TEAM

When attempting the National 3 Peaks it is advisable to have a support team of 2-4 people who are able to drive between the 3 peaks and provide the food and drinks to tired walkers. It is not advisable for walkers to both attempt the 3 peaks and drive between each area. The general tiredness of driving the long distance between each mountain and the walker's fatigue makes it essential to have a support team.

Providing food and warm drinks to walkers is very important especially in bad conditions. The last thing walkers need on returning to the foothills of each peak is to start preparing food and drinks.

Members of any support team should have some knowledge of first aid and should be able to recognise the symptoms of exposure. They should be aware of the location of the mountain rescue posts and nearest telephone for emergency. The support team should keep a spare rucksack ready to take with them in emergency with the following inside: -

- Map
- Whistle
- Survival Bag
- Spare Clothing
- Sleeping Bag
- Mobile Telephone
  (not guaranteed to function in mountainous areas).
- Compass
- Emergency Food/drink
- Notepad/Pencil
- First Aid Kit
- Torch (spare bulb/batteries)

Where possible, there should be two of the support team who are experienced and prepared to give assistance to any of the walkers in an accident/emergency situation. It may be decided that the best course of action is to go straight to the aid of a walker rather than contact the mountain rescue team initially. Any potential risks to either the injured or lost walker or the rescuer should be carefully considered before deciding your course of action.

POST WALK

After achieving your goal of walking the National 3 Peaks, whether it is in 24 hours or over a prolonged time, you may like a souvenir to mark the event. The author has produced an extensive selection of '3 peak' items, which are for sale. These are exclusive to Challenge Publications and include: - embroidered polo/T-shirts, cloth/metal badges, certificates for completing each individual peak or all 3 peaks combined, driver/support certificates and a film DVD of the route up Ben Nevis.

Due to low cloud on the summit of one or more peaks, you may not be able to take any photographs. The author has individual photo DVDs for each route, with between 140 – 220 superb photographs of the route up each mountain, with many views from the summits. These will provide a lasting souvenir or help you prepare for your walk. They can be viewed on a PC or on a television via a DVD player.

Full details are available for **all souvenirs** on our official 3 Peaks web site at **www.national3peaks.co.uk** or by sending for a current price list enclosing a S.A.E. to: -

Brian Smailes
Challenge Publications
7, Earlsmere Drive
Ardsley
Barnsley
South Yorkshire
S71 5HH

The author is compiling a register of successful attempts and would be pleased to receive names of successful walkers or any details and/or comments about your walk.

USEFUL INFORMATION

HEIGHTS OF PEAKS

Ben Nevis	1344 metres
Scafell Pike	978 metres
Snowdon	1085 metres

NEAREST MAIN TOWNS

Ben Nevis - Fort William

Scafell Pike - Keswick (northeast) Whitehaven (west) Ambleside (east)

Snowdon - Llanberis

NEAREST TELEPHONE

Ben Nevis
- Beside Glen Nevis Youth Hostel
Glen Nevis Visitor Centre
Ben Nevis Inn

Scafell
- Wasdale Head Hotel
- Farms and houses at base of Wastwater
- Seathwaite

Snowdon
- Pen-y-pass
- Llanberis
- Café on Snowdon Summit

MOUNTAIN RESCUE POSTS

Ben Nevis - Fort William Town Centre

Scafell
- Wasdale Head
- Mountain Rescue Kit near Sty Head on the Corridor Route

Snowdon
- Pen-y-pass
- Nant Peris in Pass of Llanberis

RECOMMENDED MAPS

Ben Nevis	- O.S. Explorer No.392 Ben Nevis & Fort William (1:25,000)
Scafell	- O.S. Explorer No.OL4 North west English Lakes (1:25,000)
	- O.S. Explorer No. OL6 South west English Lakes (1:25,000)
Snowdon	- O.S. Explorer No.OL17 Snowdonia (1:25,000)

WEATHER INFORMATION

Ben Nevis Area	01397 705922
	09068 500 441
Scafell Area	08700 550575
Snowdon Area	09068 500449

General Weather
www.metoffice.gov.uk   *(click on mountain weather)*

The forecast for Ben Nevis is displayed on the notice board near the start. For Snowdon, it is displayed in the window of Llanberis T.I.C. each day.

GRID REFERENCES

Ben Nevis

Glen Nevis Visitor Centre	**GR. 123730**
Glen Nevis Youth Hostel	**GR. 128718**
Halfway point on main path, near Lochan Meall An t-Suidhe	**GR. 147724**
Emergency shelter, Ben Nevis summit	**GR. 167713**

Scafell Pike

Wastwater, Wasdale Head car park	**GR. 180076**
Base of Scafell Pike	**GR. 207074**
Scafell Pike summit	**GR. 215072**
Sty Head Tarn, Corridor Route.	**GR. 221099**
Seathwaite car park, Corridor Route.	**GR. 235422**

Snowdon

Pen-y-pass (near youth hostel) car park	**GR. 648556**
Start of Llanberis Path	**GR. 581595**
Snowdon summit	**GR. 610544**

AVERAGE TIMING FOR EACH MOUNTAIN

Ben Nevis

Visitor Centre start to summit	4 hours
Summit to Visitor Centre	2¾ hours
Youth Hostel start to summit	3¾ hours
Summit to youth hostel	2¾ hours

Scafell Pike

Wasdale Head start to summit	2¾ hours
Summit to Wasdale Head	2¼ hours
Seathwaite, start to summit	3¾ hours

Snowdon

Pen-y-pass, Pyg Track start to summit	2¼ hours
Summit to Pen-y-pass, returning via Miners Track	1¾ hours
Llanberis Path to summit	2½ hours
Summit to Llanberis	1¾ hours

These timings will vary depending on the skill and fitness of your party e.g. Ben Nevis can be completed in 4½ hours with ease.

SUGGESTED ITINERARY

24 Hours Challenge

1600	touch water - Fort William
1630	start base of Ben Nevis
1845	summit of Ben Nevis
2030	base of Ben Nevis
0200	start base of Scafell Pike
0445	summit of Scafell Pike
0615	base of Scafell Pike
1230	start base of Snowdon
1430	summit of Snowdon
1530	base of Snowdon
1600	touch water – Caernarfon

To achieve these times, walkers need to be fit and walk/jog at a fast pace up/down each mountain. This can lead to hypothermia, exhaustion and accidents as walkers try to achieve the 24 hour challenge. It is not recommended, as you will get a more rewarding experience following the times below, with less chance of accidents.

A Weekend Challenge - Recommended

Saturday

start	0200	Glen Nevis Visitor Centre
	0600	Ben Nevis summit
	0830	Glen Nevis Visitor Centre
start	1630	Seathwaite or Wasdale - Lake District
	2000	Scafell Pike summit
	2230	Wasdale Head

Sunday

start	0800	Pen-y-pass-Snowdon
	1015	Snowdon summit
finish	1230	Sunday Pen-y-pass car park

NATIONAL PARK/TOURIST INFORMATION CENTRES

Glen Nevis Visitor Centre	01397 705922
Fort William T.I.C. Information Line	0845 2255121
Ballachulish T.I.C.	01855 811866
Keswick Information Centre	017687 72645
Llanberis T.I.C.	01286 870765
Betws-y-Coed T.I.C.	01690 710426
Caernarfon T.I.C.	01286 672232

The following selection of accommodation for each area is not arranged in any order of priority. All are within as reasonable distance to the walking routes as possible.

ACCOMMODATION - BEN NEVIS AREA

Campsite

Glen Nevis Caravan & Camping Park   01397 702191
Glen Nevis,
Fort William

Youth Hostel / Bunkhouse

Glen Nevis Youth Hostel   01397 702336

Glen Nevis

Ben Nevis Inn (Bunkhouse)   01397 701227
Achintee, By Claggan
Fort William PH33 6TE
info@ben-nevis-inn.co.uk
www.ben-nevis-inn.co.uk

Self Catering Log Cabin & Flat

Margaret Ferguson   01397 705905
'Harland'
Glen Nevis
Fort William PH33 6ST
margeret.ferguson@googlemail.com
www.glennevislogcabins.com

Bed & Breakfast

Sandra Mackinnon   01397 702893
Constantia House,
Fassifern Road,
Fort William. PH33 6BD
constantia.house@yahoo.co.uk
www.constantiahouse.co.uk

Gill & Dave Ferguson   01397 708496
St. Anthony's Guest House
Argyll Rd
Fort William PH33 6LF
www.stanthonysfortwilliam.co.uk
welcome@stanthonysfortwilliam.co.uk

Corrie Duff Guest House
& Holiday Cottages   01397 701412
Corrie Duff
Glen Nevis
Fort William PH33 6ST
www.corrieduff.co.uk
gill@corrieduff.co.uk

Ben Nevis Guest House   01397 708817
Glen Nevis
Fort William. PH33 6PF
www.bennevisguesthouse.co.uk
stay@bennevisguesthouse.co.uk

Mrs. F. Cook   01397 705329
'Melantee'
Achintore Road
Fort William PH33 6RW

ACCOMMODATION - SCAFELL AREA

Campsites

Seathwaite Farm   017687 77394

Wasdale Head, Barn Door Shop   019467 26384
(no showers)

Wasdale Head (Nat. Trust site)   019467 26220

Youth Hostels

Wasdale Hall Youth Hostel   019467 26222

Borrowdale Youth Hostel   0870 7705706

Bed & Breakfast

Gillian Race   019467 26242
Burnthwaite Farm   (Wasdale side)
Wasdale Head
Seascale
Cumbria. CA20 1EX
burnthwaite123@aol.com

ACCOMMODATION - SNOWDON AREA

Campsite

Ty Isaf,   01286 870494

Youth Hostels

Pen-y-pass   0870 7705990

Capel Curig   0870 7705746

Llanberis   0870 7705928

Bed & Breakfast

Erw Fair   01286 872400
High Street
Llanberis LL55 4HA
www.erwfair.com
erwfair@fsmail.net

Barry & Sue Kendrick   01286 872528
Glyn Afon
72 High Street
Llanberis LL55 4HA
www.glyn-afon.co.uk
glynafon@fsmail.net

Jane & Frank Gibson   01286 872122
Plas Coch Guest House
High Street
Llanberis LL55 4HB
www.plas-coch.co.uk
reservations@plas-coch.co.uk

ATTRACTIONS IN EACH AREA

Ben Nevis Area

Crannog Cruises	01397 700714
Nevis Range Cable Cars	01397 705825
Ben Nevis Distillery	01397 702476
Ben Nevis Highland Centre	01397 704244
West Highland Museum	01397 702169
Lochaber Leisure Centre	01397 704359
'The Jacobite' Steam Train	01524 737751

Scafell Area

Keswick Launch on Derwent Water	017687 72263
Motor Museum, Keswick	017687 73757
Cumberland Pencil Museum	017687 73626
'The Theatre by the Lake' Keswick	017687 74411

Snowdon Area

Snowdon Mountain Railway	0870 458 0033
Electric Mountain	01286 870636
Llanberis Lake Railway	01286 870549
Padarn Country Park	01286 870892

LOCAL RADIO STATIONS

These are useful to get the weather forecast in each area just before you start.

Fort William

Nevis Radio on 96.6 – 102.3 FM

Lake District

Radio Cumbria on 104.1 FM

Snowdonia

The local forecast for Snowdon is displayed in the window of the Tourist Information Centre in Llanberis each day.

USEFUL ADDRESSES /TELEPHONE NUMBERS

Long Distance Walkers Association

Paul Lawrence,
15, Tamarisk Rise,
Wokingham,
Berkshire RG40 1WG
Tel 01189 790190

This association is set up to further the interests of those who enjoy long distance walking. Members receive a journal three times each year, (strider), which includes information on all aspects of long distance walking.

Web site – www.ldwa.org.uk   E-mail LDP@ldwa.org.uk

Ramblers Association

2nd Floor, Camelford House,
87-90, Albert Embankment, London SE1 7TW
Tel. 0207 3398500

Advice and information on all walking matters. Local groups hold regular meetings.

Scottish Natural Heritage
www.snh.org.uk

The Countryside Agency for England
www.countryside.gov.uk/access

The Countryside Council for Wales
www.ccw.gov.uk

Rail Services to Fort William
www.scotrail.co.uk
08457 48 49 50

Public Transport Information for Fort William
0871 2002233

Fort William Police Station
01397 702361

GLOSSARY

B&B - Bed and Breakfast.

Bearing - A degree or number of degrees set on a compass then follow the direction of travel arrow to walk on that bearing to reach your intended destination.

Beck - A stream or brook.

Burn - Scottish word meaning stream, brook, beck or watercourse.

Cairn - An ancient stone mound erected as a marker. Often modern day piles of stones that denote a path or route are referred to as cairns.

Crag - A steep rugged rock or peak.

Dyke, Dike, Ditch - Words used to denote a long ridge of earth or a water channel either raised up or below normal level.

Escape Route - Used for any emergency situation or in times of bad visibility. The main aim is to get you down to lower ground by the safest but quickest way.

Glen - Scottish word for a valley.

G.P.S. - Global Positioning System.

Grid Reference - Derived from the National grid reference system. This is used to pinpoint a place on a map by the use of letters and numbers, written as GR. _ _ _ _ _ _

Gully - A narrow channel or cleft in a rock face. May have waterfalls, can be very slippery and have vertical drops.

Kissing Gate - Swing gate that usually lets one person through it at a time by moving the gate backwards and forwards.

Loch - Scottish word for lake.

Magnetic Bearing - This is a grid bearing taken from a map and the relevant magnetic variation added to it to obtain the magnetic bearing. See relevant maps for detail of current magnetic variation.

Metalled Road - Generally known as a stone-chipping road. This term became known as the roads metal or the roads surface.

Outcrop - Part of a rock formation that protrudes from the main body of rock.

Path - A narrow path of grass, mud, stone etc. suitable for walkers. Not usually more than 2m wide.

Plateau - A wide and mainly flat area of elevated land.

Summit - The highest point of a mountain or hill.

Tarn - A small landlocked mountain lake.

T.I.C. - Tourist Information Centre.

Track - A road (possibly rough) usually wide enough for a vehicle and often leading to a farm. Usually more than 2m wide.

Trig Point - True name is triangulation pillar. These mark the summit of many mountains, but not every mountain has one. It is a small stone pillar with a number on it. The height of the mountain is taken from this point.

The route described in this book was used by the author in 2008 and believed to be correct at the time of publication. Hopefully you have enjoyed your '3 Peaks' and gained as much pleasure from it as he did. Should you wish to walk other challenging routes, please visit Challenge Publications web site at: -

www.chall-pub.co.uk

Or the new National 3 Peaks web site

www.national3peaks.co.uk

A wide selection of walking and other guides covering the UK are available including The Novices Guide to Completing The Yorkshire 3 Peaks Walk, Hadrian's Wall, The Lyke Wake Walk, John O'Groats to Lands End (Walking) and Lands End to John O'Groats (Cycling). These books, like the others produced contain everything you need to know to complete the challenge. See list in front of book.

On our web site you will find other interesting, and possibly different walks around the British Isles, which are equally as picturesque and enjoyable as this one.

Should you wish to comment on this book or give further information to help keep the book updated then please write to the address below or e-mail via the web site. An acknowledgement will be given: -

Please write to: -

Challenge Publications
7, Earlsmere Drive,
Ardsley,
Barnsley.
S71 5HH

NOTES

GOING TO THE HILLS

Copy the following form, complete it and leave with the Police, landlady, warden or support team. Request them to contact the police if you are overdue. Report your safe return to try to prevent an unnecessary rescue operation.

Name & Address Where Staying & Tel No. . . . .

. . . .

. . . .

Next of Kin, Name, Address & Tel No. . . . .

. . . .

. . . .

Route to be taken including any map references if possible

. . . .

. . . .

. . . .

Bad Weather Alternative

. . . .

. . . .

. . . .

Date of Departure . . . .

Time of Departure . . . .

Place of Departure . . . .

Estimated Time of Return . . . .

My mobile phone No. . . . .

Vehicle Reg No. . . . .

Make . . . .

Colour . . . .

Where Parked . . . .

Walking / Climbing (delete as necessary)   Number in Party . . . .